I0022605

John Letcher Patterson

Lyric Touches

John Letcher Patterson

Lyric Touches

ISBN/EAN: 9783744651837

Printed in Europe, USA, Canada, Australia, Japan

Cover: Foto ©Thomas Meinert / pixelio.de

More available books at **www.hansebooks.com**

LYRIC TOUCHES

JOHN PATTERSON

❊❊

CINCINNATI

ROBERT CLARKE & CO

1893

COPYRIGHT, 1893,
BY ROBERT CLARKE & CO.

Acknowledgment is made for their courtesy in permitting the use of copyright poems, to the Cosmopolitan, Peterson and other magazines and periodicals.

CONTENTS.

(5)

LYRIC TOUCHES.

TO POLYMNIA.

COME, and breathe me a song, O Muse,
   Who guidest a graceful pen :
Only a delicate, lyric thing,
  No epic and deep refrain.

Round the rhymes with a far bird's note
  Or sweet, wet smell of a rose,
Or a memory with tear-drops hid
  In the cadence at the close.

Treat a theme as an artist would
  A vagrant and dreamy valse,
Leaving the ear in easy strain
  And finding no echo false.

The touch of a tress on dancer's cheek
   Inspires love's deepest sigh,
So if there be a line of love,
   Just hint at a sad, big eye.

Muse, I long for a song to-day
   Writ with a tender pen,
The verses falling in fragrant shower,
   And thoughts all sweet in their rain.

THE FAN.

I DYLLIC cloud of flossy down and silk,
Like cirrus floating o'er her hand of milk,

Upon one satin side perennial traced
A landscape whence the daisies never waste:

A flock of caded sheep which never stray
The shepherd with his reed uplift to play:

A distant skulking wolf which can no harm,
And frets the timid flock with vain alarm.

The other envied side I can not see
From feathered tip unto the ivory.

More wondrous charms I ween would be
    revealed,
Its own and of my love's flush face con-
    cealed.

AT SUNSET.

A MEADOW lark is lilting in the plain,
An owl forlornly cooing from a tree
Which velvet winds are dusting lazily.
A flock of sheep agraze within the green
Sweet grass, crops daintily toward the sheen
Of dancing stream entangled in her dress
Of violets; while floats a restlessness
In toneless fugues of light above the scene.

The sun's last kiss hath sent a vivid thrill
Through all he loves. The meadow and
  the bird
Are left full strong and warm against the
  chill
Of clammy night: the thirsty sheep have
  stirred
The dim unsilvered stream and drunk their
  fill,
And dumb with dreaming, follow I the herd.

TO THE MARÉCHAL-NEIL ROSE.

THOU art like glad canary, rose,
  Thy silken leaf its plume, thy showers
  Of perfume its lay.
Thou art like summer day that glows,
Thy golden petals, golden hours
  In a bright bouquet.

Dropped from the Dawn's disheveled hair?
For as she leaves her lord's love-bed
  A flushing from his kiss,
I've seen a creamy rich rose there
Croceous-hued fall from her head,
  And thou art like to this.

Full happy are thy dimpled leaves,
For each is wed to loving mate
  Nor dying lie apart.
As yellow wheat bound into sheaves
They cling together and await
  On one another's heart.

Thou livest only summer's length,
And canst not bear the birds' good-bye
　　Like the asters cold.
The sun must woo thee in his strength,
Or in modest rains thy scents reply
　　While the tale is told.

What if thy cup of life is small?
Who would not long for beaker brimmed
　　With such cordial wine,
A draught which blends the sweets of all,
And then to rest with requiem hymned
　　By birds, O rose divine!

TWO SIGHS.

ONE sigh for a song,
  For a song that is sung.
It was sung me erst long
Was the song.

And one for a rose,
For a rose whilom white.
It is faded to-night,
Is the rose.

Love sang me the song,
And love gave me the flower
In a long vanished hour,
Rose and song.

And so will I sigh—
It is all love has left :
When in thought I'm adrift
Will I sigh.

THE PARIAH.

NO music has softened the din of her
     day—
The night which approaches brings music
    for aye.

The roses are wan in the way she has
    trod—
In freshness they bloom on the grave's
    narrow sod.

No peace has she found in the path of the
    past—
Adown by the cypress she finds peace at
    last.

And sorrow is fled, burning tears cease
    their flow—
" Thy sins though as scarlet, shall be white
    as snow."

A WINTER HEMP-FIELD.

THE men returning from the valley
    fields
Of hemp are singing near the tilted bars
  A strange, wild tune.
The tin-pails swinging from their sturdy
    arms
Twinkle with silver faces of vain stars
  And slender moon.

The breaks, like oxen from the harness free,
Stand wan with moon-light and their duty's
    dust,
  Ghostly and mute.
And crisply crack the scattered sheaves of
    hemp —
Slim lances ready for the morrow's joust—
  To parting foot.

The fires are fading of the burning shives,
The embers waken from their ashy swoon
  In cloudy pipes.

The carts go rattling down the roseless
　　lane,
Apast the orchard which presents no boon
　　To thirsty lips.

Fainter than distance grows the homing
　　throng
Of workmen singing, and the neighing
　　team,
　˙ Over the hill.
Softer than shadow is the breast of Peace
Brooding and nestling with the pale moon-
　　gleam
　　Over the dell.

God-Nature's workmen have begun their
　　task.
Their steel aglitter gives no clamorous time
　　Nor martial sound.
They pierce the hemp hearts with their
　　silver blades
Of frost, and fetter with the rings of rime
　　The captive ground.

These curious workmen carve their cameos
Into the onyx of the frozen field
  By evening's lamp.
Mysterious cryptograms which puzzle him
Who . saw this thing within a winter field
  Of the tented hemp.

WOULD!

A FULL camellia at her breast,
　　As white and cold
As if of snow-flakes matched and held
　　In frozen fold.

A flower of haughty beauty pure·
　　But no perfume.
More suited dead than living heart,
　　The scentless bloom.

What if her heart is free of love's
　　Perfume as this?
And if her lips so beautiful
　　Are cold to kiss?

Would that the white camellia
　　To red rose turn!
Would that the warmest flame of love
　　Her dear heart burn!

ΕΙΣ ΧΕΛΙΔΟΝΑ.

(From Anakreon.)

THOU, dear Swallow,
　　Coming once a year
Dost braid thy nest in summer,
　　In winter disappear
　　. To Memphis or the Nile.
But Love is ever braiding
　　Its nest within my heart,
And Love's egg is waiting,·
　　When Love is winged to part,
　　　Nearly hatched the while.
So the gaping birdies'
　　Cries are heard alway.
The grown Loves feed the Lovelings;
　　No sooner fledged than they
Are busy hatching others—
　　What hope is then for me?
My strength is insufficient
　　Such countless Loves to flee!

COMRADES.

A BAND of comrades have I,
    A chosen band of three
Who tend my daily marches
    And guard the tent of me.

He strong, with girded. loins,
    With shining shield and mail
And bow and arrow ready,
    Is my brave warrior " Will."

And often when the battle
    Is loud with hue and strife,
And I am faint and failing,
    His arm protects my life.

He swift, with piercing vision,
    . And keen axe at his side,
With steps secure and steadfast,
    Is " Truth " my trusty guide.

And if when deep bewildered
In ways unknown and new
I grasp his honest fingers,
He leads me safely through.

She sweet, with harp and psaltery,
With eyes like summer shade
And voice of low bells linking,
Is " Hope " my fair handmaid.

And she, when I am wounded,
With balsam from her breast
Binds up my bleeding sinews
And soothes my soul to rest.

And so wherever tented,
Their fearless fires are here,
And I secure from danger,
My comrades bivouacked near.

THE HANDKERCHIEF.

EXQUISITE, airy thing
    Linen and lace,
Soft as a white dove's wing,
    Brushing her face.

Pure as the tea-rose bloom,
    Queen of its band,
Holding the light perfume
    Caught from her hand.

Bordered with slender lines
    Silken, and cleft
Fine as the spider twines
    Into his weft.

This is the handkerchief
    Delicate, sweet,
Fallen like lily-leaf
    Down by her feet.

A HYMN..

WHEN no hand helping
    In waters foaming
Life seemeth waning,
Thou art my Rope.
When eyes are weary,
When days are gloaming,
Still art Thou near me,
    Jesu, my Hope.

When I a wanderer
Proud through the passes
Slip into pit-falls,
Thou art my Crook.
When I a doubter
See through dark glasses,
Thou comest nearer,
    Jesu, my Book.

Sound of the sobbing
Left for the living
This can not reach me,

When on Thy breast.
Groans of the failing,
Groans of the striving,
Will be earth-echoes,
   Jesu, my Rest.

White let them robe me
Meet for Thy pity,
Lilies to plead with
Their breath, mine lost.
   Into Thy kingdom,
     Beautiful City,
       Jesu, receive me,
       Jesu, my Host.

THE WISH.

(At Love's Birth.)

CLEAR, tender star of evening
    hour,
  Be thou as Olden Star a guide,
Perform for me thy fabled power,
    And lead his foot-steps to my side.
The over-curving crest of heaven
    Without thy blue would be but
      dim,
And as thy blue to perfect heaven,
    Is he to me, and I to him.

Clear, tender star of evening hour,
    Be thou as Olden Star a guide,
And when thou shinest on my bower
    Restrain thy course and here abide.
I care not if he brings no treasure
    Like Eastern princes took with
      them.
No gold can pay the price of pleasure
    Is he to me, and I to him.

DARK.

L AST night the mystery of dark within
      A tiny heart untried of grief was born
And baby-lips by sorrow's sobs unworn.
A mother's anguish paid the greed of pain.

Last night beneath the shivering, pallid stars
A snowy head and faded face were dead;
From weary heart the agony was fled,
The late soul lifted o'er the Golden Bars.

Oh! mystery of dark, of flowing tears!
To-night, to-morrow will it still repeat?
Shall no last breath soon earth's design
      complete,
Or shall Time's tarnish dim unnumbered
      years?

Hath not a sculptor carved a marble fame
Divine enough to catch immortal flush?
Hath never painter touched a face to blush
With life fulfilling the Creator's aim?

Hath poet never strung the purposed shell
And never sung the tuneful song of songs?
Among the aeons' countless beauty-throngs
Hath perfect woman never woven spell?

When o'er this pulseless breast blue violets
    move,
For they will wave feeling my heart in
    them,
Shalt thou be born, the long-awaited Brahm,
To prove all creeds are right in truth of
    love?

Beneath this cypress to the marble mark
From, in yon chamber, woman's travail cry,
This one way we are passing you and I :
Who seek to see beyond find ever—dark!

AD PUERUM.

(From Horace.)

I HATE the Persian pageant, boy,
  Rich chaplets twined with bark
    annoy.
Forbear to seek where haply yet
  The wild-rose linger late.

A simple myrtle wreath prepare;
On nothing else bestow a care,
For while I quaff 'neath clustered vine,
  It suits my brow and thine.

LOVE AND FANCY.

I HID my heart
     In a radiant rose of red—
A flower flushed with its touch—
     Lone charm in my tangled bed.

To Fancy brought,
     The flower was left to die,
Idly breathing its tale.
     Forgotten flower and I.

At last Love finds
     And binds the rose in her breast.—
I laugh at Fancy's form
     As Love is tenderly pressed.

A PÆAN.

THEY have taken from Zeus his scepter,
  They have banished Bel from his
    throne.
They would drive my God from His Heaven
  And leave me to die alone.

But I gaze on His splendid palace,
  And His eloquent envoys there,
The sky with its stars of silver,
  And I fancy no foolish fear.

I look on His works of wonder,
  The earth, the sea and the sun,
And the work portrays the Master,
  Which none but He could have done.

Let them marshal their hosts to battle,
  I'll brighten my helm and shield.
And I know that in spite of their taunting
  Jehovah shall win the field.

WHEN TO-MORROW SHALL BE TO-DAY.

W HEN to-morrow shall be to-day;
     When the night shall be wept away,
Will the kindly sun make dry our tears,
As he dries the dews from the rose which
     dares
To lift her blushing face to be kissed?
Will the night's long anguish fade with its
     mist
     When to-morrow shall be to-day?

When to-morrow shall be to-day;
When the silvern stars grow gray,
And the herd to the distant hill departs,
Will the morning lark bring the song to
     hearts
Which he brings to the depths of throbbing
     shy?
As he sings serenely, shall you and I
     When to-morrow shall be to-day?

When to-morrow shall be to-day ;
When winter hours drift into May,
When bird and sweetheart are building a
    nest,
Will love return to the empty breast?
Will the same clear eyes again beguile,
Enchanting still with the old sweet smile,
When to-morrow shall be to-day ?

When to-morrow shall be to-day ;
When the clay shall return to clay ;
When we to the Master Death are thrall,
And willows are weeping over all,
Will our sorrow sink in the River of Rest,
Will our names be numbered among the
    best
    When to-morrow shall be to-day ?
    When all to-morrows shall be to-day ! !

OVER A PICTURE.

SWEET girl, I love thee for thy face
Where truth and beauty find a place
To dwell with purity—a mien
Of Poesy's conceit hast thou—
In Grecian mind thou must have been
A goddess meant for Parian snow.
God took the thought, and chiseled thee
From his divine and throbbing clay.

Above the pictured face I dream
And look until mine eyes grow dim—
Her features blend into a blot.
My heart's cold altar of desire,
Her eye, a flame forget-me-not,
Shall light forever with pure fire.
And with those heaven-tender eyes
A heart shall burn its sacrifice.

THE BUTTERFLY AND ROSE.

A BUTTERFLY of weary wing
  Flew to a rose to rest and swing.

The butterfly, a bloom of light,
The rose was only snowy white.

"Am I not fair, O rose," said he,
" The rainbow scarce can fairer be.

" See where the gold to orange turns,
And purple kissed by crimson burns.

"A flower taught to fly; a gem
In azure air to float and gleam.

"And like a falling star my flight;
While thou art only simple white."

I weened the taunt while passing by,
And for the rose did make reply.

"A worm art thou on painted wings,
The bud is white from which she springs."

AUTUMN LEAVES.

A UTUMN leaves of the forest,
    Ye are letters woven strong
Into tales of the scarlet woman
    In her revel and her song.

Ye were modest in maid's sweet manner,
    And your songs were pure and divine.
Now your words are wild with passion,
    And your lips are aglow with wine.

Ye came, and the sun came burning,
    Defiling you with his gold,
As a lover kisses with laughter
    Such lips as are bought and sold.

TO-MORROW..

THERE is a maiden light and fair,
    With hint of sunshine on her hair.
Her deep eyes flash so dark a blue
That by them sapphires lose their hue.

Around her throngs a fairy band
Of Hopes all dancing hand in hand;
While grim old Time, with locks of snow
Is playing for them where they go.

And crowds of lovers vain pursue
The Circe maid with eyes of blue,
For if to kiss her any tries,
With mocking laugh to Time she flies.

To-morrow is the maiden's name
Whose looks the hearts of men inflame,
Who in the path of death beguiles
Still beckoning with seductive smiles.

IN MEMORY OF SUMMER.

WHERE doth the brimming rose spill
      musk
     Along the way,
     Where whitely stray
The smooth bare feet, at dew of dusk,
Of maiden to the spring, her throat
Repeating softer tones than rote
From tremulous harp wind-strung?
Songs of thy sweetness sung,
     Roseal Summer.

Dreary these dim and tearful days
     When ravaged glades
     Wear tattered shreds,
And sadly hangs a crape-like haze
Upon the wistful woods unleaved,
While to thy memory, bereaved
Thy voice a dervish song
In many a mystic tongue
     Mourning thee, Summer.

When mocking winds are flaunting snow
     On meadows
     Which they froze,
I wonder where thy warm winds flow
Scented with floating blossom-shells,
Sweetly fluctuate to thy calls
And flower-fingered hand,
And where the blue-bird band
     Lilts to thee, Summer ?

If I were where thy lilies sigh
     In perfumed prayers
     Unto the stars,
Their sainted kindred of the sky,
Could they and birds retune my heart
To gladder mood and happier art ;
Have my dear hopes outflown
Thy scepter and thy throne,
     Summer, sweet Summer ?

AN IDOL.

THERE are pearls like those of the cir-
    cling sea
Whiter than beads of milk can be.
But they must be gained with glittering gold,
For pearls like the shivering sea are cold.

There are two sapphires blinding blue
Like pieces of sky which have fallen through,
But a palace's luster must light the gems,
For in a cottage no sapphire gleams.

There are twin rubies of warmer red
Than breasts of robins by arrows bled.
But only mammon can kiss their ray,
Remote as the distant stars from me.

And these fair gems in an idol are
That will crush me under her cruel car.
For others are offering riches rife,
And I can offer but love and life.

THE VINAIGRETTE.

A N incensed fane
     By silvery chain
    There swings :
A gleaming mold
Where cling in gold
    Strange things.

The good Koran
Doth damn the man
    Who spun
The dragon wings,
And beasts and things
    Thereon.

And yet this rest
Of bird and beast
    In rows
The girl I woo
Keeps lifting to
    Her nose ;

And out and in
The stopper thin
    She draws,
Her hands retrace
From lap to face
    Because

This temple-tray
Ammonia
    Conceals—
This silhouette
A vinaigrette
    Reveals.

A PRAYER.

OH! come to my sorrow,
   Peace, like the calm to the sea,
And bring to the haunted darkness
   Light from eternity.

Keep watch on my mourning,
   Stars of the steel bright beams,
And send from the realm of heaven
   Hope with her peaceful dreams.

Attune to my comfort,
   O Lyre of Heavenly Love,
And perch on my burthened bosom,
   Rest, like the white Ghost-Dove.

Oh! come, gentle Slumber,
   Press thy sweet lips to my eyes,
And whisper like a mother crooning,
   The promise of Paradise.

UNDER THE ASPENS.

THE minstrel-wind's love touch hath made
  The gleaming bosom of the lake
To palpitate in sweet alarm.
The aspen trees resent the kiss
The saucy reveler gave, trembling
Musically to eye and ear.
While silvery leaves beam like faint stars,
And twinkle in the tender blue.

A careless dreamer lies beneath
The milky-way of leaves, and loves
To hear the tales the poplars tell—
How such a lover said, "I love,"
And carved within their snowy peel
Two names he would were one.

WITH THE ROBINS' SONG.

SWEET is the robins' vesper song
    Which melts in the blaze of golden sky,
  As the sun goes down and the birds fly by
And come in the maize with their melody,

Where the purple corn-flowers cling
    Close to the stalks of the withering maize,
    Like memories cling to fading days
And bloom in the heart in the evening haze.

With breasts as red as the mellow peach
    And red throats rounded with songs out-
      pour
    They seem ripe fruits as the day is o'er,
And corn to bear what the peach-trees bore.

The reapers rest on their silvery scythes
    Or silently lie on the heaps of husk,
    While from the dimbles of corn, the
      musk
Of flowers and the robins' song in the dusk.

Sing on, suave birds, in the crested corn,
　When the day is done and the night is nigh
　May I have hymned such a melody
As yours to pierce to the purple sky!

SUB QUO CŒLO?

WHO says that summer has no snow?
    Look at the rose-buds in summer-
  hair,
Fragrant snow-flakes floating there
Into the white drift of her brow.

Who says no flowers the ice-lands grace?
    Look at the violets liquid blue
    Staining me purple through and through,
In the Frigid Zone of her frowning face.

I know not if the summer 's gone:
    I know not if the winter be:
    The twice two seasons are mixed for me
Who follow the moods of this fairest one.

THE SOUL.

THINE eyes are clear with soul therein.
   Beneath the laces of the lash
There shines a light pure as is seen
   In reflex of a brilliant's flash.

And as the sunbeam lights the stone
   And lends its luster to the gem,
So too thine eyes' light 's not their own ;
   The soul it is which shines in them.

IN THE AUTUMN WOOD.

THE autumn-wounded bleeding wood
    Draws close around its cloak of mist
        To hide the clinging blood.

The red leaves fly against my face
With slender claws of fir and pine,
        Like birds intruders chase.

A sunbeam weary of its flight
Lies panting on the maple's breast,
        A languid shape of light.

Or is it a last butterfly
Softly waving with rainbow wings,
        This envoy of the sky?

Yon late flower seems in its retreat
An alabaster vase of spice,
        Broken at Autumn's feet.

Invisible its odors fly
In rapid rings of spikenard sweet
    Into the purple sky.

I feel their light touch on my face,
As when we feel the silken sweep
    Of wings in some dim place.

What faint far birds are those which sing
Like hopes of summer trouped for rout,
    Like dreams on waking wing?

Their music sets my fancy free.
I hear the oaten pipe of Pan
    In sylvan minstrelsy.

Strange dryads roam the darkling wood
And deep illusive eyes delude
    Of Faun and forest-god.

I pull with them the flammeous grape;
I crush wild wine of memory
    Until my pulses leap.

I live again the happy time
When earth was all a singing-place,
    And love my only rhyme.

And now the heavy gloom of care
Is on the autumn's wings of haze
    Floating, fading, lost in air.

DURING A SONATA.

THE music-perfume poured around me
    makes
The very soul within me drunk,
While she is playing in a fragrant sea
Of liquid notes the wimble fire of art
Diffuses into scented harmony.

She holds my heart in her white restless
    hands,
And would a melody it were,
That she interpret its impassioned strain!
For then her ear would harken to the plea,
Which trembles at its pink approach in vain.

WITH A FOUR-LEAVED CLOVER.

THERE is a tender little flower
    So meek, so soft with sympathy,
They cling together happily
In a scented circlet-portraiture
Of sixty minutes in the hour
I spent upon their drowsy bed,
To wreathe bands for her burnished head
And find Hap's four-leaved clover flower.

The mead and I miss each of them;
The bumble-bee waits for their sweet.
My four-leaved clover faded, dim
With me I offer at her feet.
Do I wake or do I dream?
She makes my happiness complete!

TO THE MOUNTAIN MIST.

(The Alleghanies, 1892.)

M IST that clings so soft
       To the green lace upon the mountain's
    breast,
With downy wings sky-sent
To brood the beauty of the rocks divest,
Far on thy pinions blue
My soul would fly with thee, empyreal mist.

Forgetful of cold reason
My rhyme would bear my soul in mystery
Dissolving in thy vapor;
A soul to dream such volant dreams as fly
From reason's hardening hands,
Like smoke-designs in artist-fingers die.

Diffused in glyns and dingles;
Glad as the wild-grape wine's unravished
    mirth;
Part of air's purity

My soul would float to-day from sorrow's
    dearth—
A wish thy Weirds are laughing
As old as longing and their purple birth!

A SERENADE.

BUDS of the lily-Graces
Hiding their snowy faces
Weary resisting, languidly lie.
The lover current is kissing,
Kissing and closely pressing
His lips to their love-pale lips with a sigh.

Sweet, I float in the flowers
Under the silvern shores.—
What if the lune and the lilies are fair?
Silverest moon is dreary,
Whitest pond-lilies weary
Until my lily, my love is here.

Soon will the moon be shaded,
Soon will lilies be faded,
The water will darken, the warmness be
cold.
Come ere the lilies wither,
List to my plaining zither,
Come ere the night and we grow old.

FATE.

TWO birds go singing over head,
  Two swallows swift and sweet.
Their glad love lay makes melody
  While day and darkness mate.

They build their nest in a mossy ruin
  Whose guests have long been dead,
And gaily chirp in the solitude
  Of halls no foot-falls thread.

For some must hush for some to sing,
  And joy comes after grief.
Palace will mold, but nest will build,
  And death createth life.

TO A SLIPPER.

IN the dream of the languous valse
    Softly circle
Silver with sheen of the silver light,
    Slender slipper,
When the touch of her tiny foot falls,
Kissing its shadow as day does night.

In the mutable maze lead my love
    Lightly, smoothly
As swallow sailing o' evening late,
    Burnished slipper,
Like the down of a tremulous dove
Winging, gleaming by with its mate.

In the drift of the vagrant valse
    Slowly circle,
Hiding the heart which I place in thine,
    Silken slipper,
Ere the weight of her proud foot falls
Crushing cruelly, knowing it mine.

AN AUTUMN SONG.

IN the wood
   Autumn presses her wine,
Till the flood
Overpours every tree and vine,
Staining leaves and the golden weed
With sardoin and sulphur shine.

   In the hills
Flutters the falling leaf.
   It appeals
To my heart as a symbol of grief,
Sinking down in the breast of the wind
Which gusts over stubble and sheaf.

   In the air
Are strange echoes and murmurings.
   From the bare
Bush where yon late bird swings
And sings, are the leaves awhirl
Like a covey of birdless wings.

Ere thy flight
Bird, why sing—if bird thou art,
Not a sprite,
Nor a fancy of autumn's heart.
Thinkest thou the foot-falls of woe
From the wood at song will depart?

And I am
Dazed at hearing thee sing.—
In my dream
And the mystic visions which spring
In the heart at the fall of the leaf,
When the roses are withering.

So farewell!
No other singing, nor thine
Can dispel
The mist from the hill and the sign
Of sorrow which is set in the wood,
In days of the summer's decline.

U. T
LIVE
C.

TO-DAY.

THE swarth night draws his eager cur-
tains low
About the gold locks of the winsome west.
The hint provokes a holy passion-glow
When day's divest.

I long to couch me with this sweet to-day
Who rambled through the rosies sunnily,
If this pure wife might haply gender me
Such heirs as she.

TO A FALLEN LEAF.

THE happy summer lived with thee,
   Happy with bloom and bird returned,
Now all thy beauty blear and burned,
The weeping summer dies with thee.
The autumn's winds low threnody,
   A dirge for all thy kindred mourned,
   Sighs o'er thy fallen form un-urned
Beneath the forest's feet to lie.

But soon will snow with silent hand
   Spread crystal wreaths and winding sheet;
And tears adorn thee and thy band
   Beneath whose tarnished coronet
Many a narrow mound will stand,
   Where happiest summers terminate.

SUB ROSA.

I HAVE fallen in love with a rose
  And have plighted my faith to hers
For her sweetness when I was sad
  And her tender responsive tears.

She had wept all the night, as I,
  At such sorrows we have, not you
Who laugh at the fanciful griefs
  Which a rose and a dreamer know.

I have gathered the rose to my heart:
  But, rose, is my love so true
Since you fell from the careless breast
  Of a lady more fair than you?

A CLUSTER OF GRAPES.

M ISTY-purple globes,
 Beads which brown autumn
   strings
Upon her robes,
Like amethyst ear-rings
Behind a bridal veil
Your veils of bloom their gems reveal.

    Mellow, sunny-sweet
Ye lure the banded bee
    To juicier treat,
Aiding his tipsy spree
With more dulcet wine
Than clover white or wild woodbine.

    Dripping rosy dreams
To me of happy hall
    Where laughter trims
The lamps till swallow-call;
Of flowery cup and throng
Of men made gods in wit and song.

Holding purer days
Your luscious fruitfulness,
  When prayer and praise
The bleeding ruby bless,
And memory sees the blood
Of Christ the Savior, God and good.

Monks of lazy hills,
Stilling the rich sunshine
  Within your cells,
Teach me to have such wine
Within my breast as this
Of faith, of song, of happiness.

r

VERSE.

FOOLISH we think to make our verses bright
By writing ruby, diamond, sapphire, gem.
Foolish we fear to make our verses dim
By writing rust, tarnish, cloudy, trite.
Carping his song retards no swallow's flight;
Singing of summer maketh sprout no as-
    phodel;
Calling it dark opaques no crystal well;
Calling it crystal sweets no brackish bight.

The age is of form-verses, not of power.
We strive to philter muses with such herbs
Of speech, as witch ne'er demon with the
    lure
Of plants so sapless. Let the magic herbs
Of rhythm, pungent and powerful conjure
The Nine in fewer adjectives, more verbs.

THE EPIPHANY.

CHRIST, Thou art born; Thy star is in
the sky.
'I seem to see three camels tread the plain
Laden with precious gold and nard again
At the new symbol of Epiphany.
Perchance the magi from death's swathes
are free,
Their limbs unmuffled from the spicy fold,
The stones from off their crumbling
couches rolled
To suffer them again to worship Thee.

Jesus Savior, keep our vision clear,
And make our souls from faithless dark-
ness free
To see in Heaven always thy guiding star,
Always the light of thy Epiphany;
That the fainter grow the scenes of earth
and far,
The fairer grow our sense of Heaven and
.   Thee.

TO THE STARS.

TREMULOUS slaves of the light,
  Blue and silver and white,
    At glance of the moon,
Stars, are ye pale with fright?

Are your beams buds in a spray,
Bloom of ethereous sea
    Which maidens hold
Glad in eternity? ﹡

Or gems in the angel's breast,
Bearing dead souls to rest
    Unto heaven—
Gems of his lucent vest.

Secret my soul would know
Flashes to me below:
    " Learn that we are
Eyes of the gods on you!"

TO A MOCKING BIRD.

WHEN the slender shallop of the moon
　　Glides among the lights on the azure
　sea,
Propelled by sails unseen and winds un-
　　known,
Dashing softly earthward a silver spray,
　Wakeful thou art singing dreamily.

All not beautiful is now unseen
Beneath the silver-plating of the spray.
The white-robed Earth swings incense from
　　her fane,
And silent are the choristers for thee
　　To chant the lesson of thy ecstasy.

Brown-surpliced prelate of flowery glade,
The interwoven notes of melody
Which loudly fill thy ruffled throat or fade
And faint adagio from tree to tree
Were made for such a night, the night for
　　thee.

Fragrant almost is thy minstrelsy :
I scarcely know which sense receives the
     bliss ;
I hear it, smell it with the apple tree
And even feel it with the breezes' kiss,
    So all-pervading is its tenderness.

The ocean ever singeth to the exiled shell :
Far summers echo in thy plaintive lay
Which seems to hold the music and the
     smell
Of scenes of many a vanished June and
     May,
    Kept as shells keep the memory of the sea.

Holy, holy is each phantasy
Awakened by thy song—a prayer more true
Than any Christian ever sent on high.
And peace and calmness follow thy adieu,
    As the pure orison transcends the blue.

AN OLD MAID.

THROUGH warmer glows of girlhood
    days
She meekly passed, her love conceived
Immaculate.   Her soft heart grieved,
Still bleeds with flowing sympathies.
A noble woman she portrays
The sensitive soul misunderstood,
The hungry heart starving for food,
The woman wronged of love and praise.

What if no mesh of scarlet cheeks,
No lure of eyes, nor silken tress
Detain beauty captive ?   Who seeks
The soul heeds not its humble dress.
The sweetness of her smile bespeaks
Pure beauty born of saintliness.

UNDER A PICTURE.

THE lamplight faints and croons the
　　fire's flame,
Then pagan silence rests my chairs among.
Above the mantel hangs an oaken frame—
Love smiles on kneeling me idolatrous.

An oaken frame with wreath of silver
　　sheaves—
Faunus did carve the wooden thing for me,
And twisted to the rim some slender leaves
Which frost had mellowed with a soft white
　　fire.

Her image pensive through a circled glass.
She looked one moon into a mirror-pool;
The loving waters crystallized her face,
And Cupid cut this picture in the disc.

Faunus and Cupid! did these twain recall
That I had mocked the old gods as a dream?
Now is a goddess in my heathen hall,
Bright face of heaven in a temple dim.

ΕΙΣ ΡΟΔΟΝ.

(From Anakreon.)

O ROSE of the Loves,
   Let us steep it in wine,
The beauty-leaved rose
Round our temples entwine
While we drink, while we smile
   Rose, fairest flower,
   Boast of spring's bower,
Even gods you beguile.
   And Cythera's boy
Twists the rose in his hair
   As he leads on the dance
   With the Graces to share.
Crown me then while I play,
   O Bacchus to thee:
Round thy shrine, god of wine,
   With a deep-bosomed girl,
Rosy wreaths on my brow,
   I shall whirl, I shall whirl.

UNDER THE MISTLETOE.
(To E. H.)

A THOUGHT'S span holding mistletoe
Gathered from the braw oak's breast—
The sun's orbed fire seems altar flame,
The wrinkled oak a Druid priest.

Silently I bend my head
Until the Druid cease to pray
And chant to beads of mistletoe
Ancient Briton carmina.

The mistletoe hath green gold pins
Where pearls of waxen berries glow :
Such things as hold a lady's hair—
What if my love should stand below ?

With brown large eyes where darkness haunts
As in the deep of dreamy stream ;
Her braided hair in curves and curls
With just enough of gold to gleam.

I 'd kneel me on the happy leaves
   Trembling and warm beneath her feet,
And gentle draw her down beside
   Until the forfeit were complete.

The oak tree sighs; remembers he
   The vine which clung about his breast
And twined love-flowers into his locks?
   Make I and Druid one request?

I wonder if his god more kind,
   Or he a tenderer prayer can pray,
And if the Druid wins his wish
   Which God Jehovah grants not me?

TO A STRING OF PEARLS.

WHITE weal of the sea
 Cling tenderly
As I, if I thus were blest.
 Smoother than silk
 Of first dews of milk
Which shine on the pinks of a breast.

 Is each a gem
 Which once did gleam
From lips like the sard for red?
 Cold in the grave
 Which pale tides lave
With froth and the wan sea-weed.

 Strung on a strand
 Of floss as bland
As tresses of red, red gold,
 Pearls, were ye thread
 From dead lips and head
As the moaning waves have told?

FAITH.

HE gathers all his squadrons some brave
    day
He, Youth, commanding, and his captain
    Hope.
Ambition, Faith, Love rally on the slope
Which lifts unto the enemy's array.
Bold cavalry with restless sword and steed,
The banners curling and the bugles blown,
Thy flash, thy courage and thy might are
    thrown
Up hill into a fatal enfilade.

Life's batteries unmask with many a gun;
And thick hail hurtles the impulsive band:
Love's sabre falters ere the summit's won;
Ambition wounded wails his nerveless hand.
But Faith stands on the envied height alone,
Spikes the last gun and waves his bannered
    wand.

NOCTURNE.

THERE trembles near my starlit way
  A timid rose
Which seems a fragrant flake of snow
  That summer brings
Back to the air whence winter tore the spray.

The white shell dropeth a pearl-tear
  When it is culled:
This rose which knows her not is sad,
  And I'd be glad
To die upon her beauty's buds or hair.

Sadly I listen where he flies
  In path of song
To mocking-bird I startle doomed to die
  Within the lake,
Mistaking its clear mirror for the skies.

But as I cross the lichened bars
  Into the lane,
I smile to hear some love-lorn lad
  To slender maid
Swearing her bright tender eyes are stars.

I wander till far worlds grow faint
        And fainter grow,
Until their gray blends with day skies,
        And morning birds
Mock at my singing with a mild complaint.

THOU.

(To E. H.)

D USK gold of scented hair thy coronet,
  Twisted and tangled with a careless
    care,
Clinging about thy temples smooth and fair
As some pure things the snow confesses
    white.
And when thy mysteries of deep eyes speak
Rebuke, soft with their wounded tenderness,
Enchanted I with beauty's holiness
Stagger like one between the dream and
    wake.

With sard and alabaster of thy face
Give of thy mouth the pearl and coral red,
And let these gems my happy cottage grace;
Then men shall point of me when I am
    dead:
" Behold! a miser lived in yonder place,
And in his heart was all his treasure hid!"

WHEN.

WHEN laughter flew
  My world wide through
Glad winged as homing, happy dove,
  And autumn's flail
  Swept summer's trail,—
  I asked my love.

When her brown eyes
Shown bright as is
The seven-toned light from worlds above,
  And Youth's pen traced
  Life's etchings chaste,—
  I blessed my love.

When her dear eyes
Are wet as lies
A deep, deep pool while rain-drops rove,
  And sorrow halts
  Within their vaults,—
  God keep my love!

When clear light flies
My love's big eyes,
As bird will leave his chosen nest,
When we are old
My heart shall fold
And love her best.

THE SILENT GATES.

THROUGH the silent gates
There comes the slow, sweet breath
    Of roses dozing,
And whispered intercourse
    Of wind and leaves.

There the shadows fall
Like wings of weary birds
    Feebly fluttering,
Till sunbeams cover them
    With nets of gold.

Through the silent gates
There comes the quick coarse cry
    Of ravens calling,
And the sodden sound
    Of falling clay.

There the marble doors
Display their snow in which
    Are traced sad legends
And the carven names
    Of guests within.

There our sleepers sleep—
And you and I who wake ·
         Beyond the grating
Of the silent gates
         Are drowsy, waiting.

CHORAL ODE.

(Euripides' Medea, lines 627-662.)

THE Loves in excess bring nor virtue
    nor fame,
But if Cypris gently should come,
No goddess of heaven so pleasing a dame:
Yet never, O mistress, in sure passion
    steeped,
Aim at me thy gold bow's barbéd flame.

May temperance watch o'er me, best gift of
    the gods,
May ne'er to wild wrangling and strifes
Dread Cypris impel me soul-pierced with
    strange lust;
But with favoring eye on the quarrelless
    couch
Spread she wisely the love-beds of wives!

Oh fatherland! Oh native home!
Never city-less
May I tread the weary path of want

Ever pitiless
And full of doom;
But on that day to death, to death be slave!
Without a country's worse than in a grave.

Mine eye hath seen, nor do I muse
On other's history.
Nor home nor friend bewails thy nameless
pangs.—
Perish dismally
The fiend who fails
To cherish friends, turning the guileless key
Of candor's gate! Such friend be far from
me!

www.ingramcontent.com/pod-product-compliance
Lightning Source LLC
Chambersburg PA
CBHW031449270326
41930CB00007B/924

9 7 8 3 7 4 4 6 5 1 8 3 7